The Handbook for Effective Job Development

Placing the Hard-to-Employ in the Private Sector

Samuel R. Connor
Mary Beth Pelletier
Original Contributions by David J. Rogers

CHICAGO RESEARCH AND TRADING GROUP, LTD.
440 SOUTH LA SALLE STREET
CHICAGO, ILLINOIS 60605

9/14/87
ow

Work in America Institute, Inc.
Scarsdale, New York

The material for this publication is produced as part of Contract #99-9-2072-33-32 for the U.S. Department of Labor.

Printed in the United States of America.

Purchase Information:

Quantity	Price
1-4	$14.95
5-24	13.50
25-99	12.00
100-499	11.00
500 or more	10.00

Prices are subject to change. To order, write to the Publications Department, Work in America Institute, Inc., 700 White Plains Road, Scarsdale, New York 10583. Please allow 4-6 weeks for delivery.

Preface

If you are a Job Developer working to place hard-to-employ youth in the private sector, then this handbook is written for you.

The purpose of the book is to help to make you more effective in your efforts to place and retain young workers in permanent entry-level jobs. Whether you are new to your job or have many years of experience, the book will provide you with a variety of ways for improving your operation.

The handbook is intended to be a practical guide to the real world of the job developer. The methods and techniques presented are those used by a number of successful agencies. They have been tried and found to be effective. While some techniques may not be directly applicable to your agency, most can be adapted to particular situations. As you read, keep this in mind and avoid discounting any method until you have given it a full test.

Contents

Your Role
As A Job Developer

Overview

You have probably discovered by now that being successful as a job developer takes dedication, energy and a clear understanding of what is expected of you. While you are undoubtedly clear on the first two attributes, you may have some questions about the specific details of your job.

To clarify this, we will use the role concept approach to define your job. This newer approach to job definition addresses active job behaviors, rather than the more passive responsibilities and duties. This approach adds a dimension of understanding not possible with the traditional job description.

The intent of this first chapter is to help you gain the best possible understanding of your job and what is expected of you. The chapter is intended to be descriptive only. The chapters that follow will discuss the details of each role.

The Role Concept

For years, personnel departments have used job descriptions to define jobs. These descriptions took the form of a list of duties and responsibilities assigned to a particular position. Today, these passive descriptions are giving way to the modern role concept, which defines the job in terms of the active roles necessary to perform effectively. The net effect is to provide the job holder with a better idea of what is expected of him and, as a result, lower the level of frustration and increase the level of effectiveness.

The Five Roles of a Job Developer

The basic function of a job developer is to find potential employers, determine their employment needs and place qualified job applicants with that employer. Doing this job requires a variety of activities that fall under five major roles. Depending upon your agency and its organizational structure, the importance of these roles can vary. In nearly every case, however, the first three will always be of prime importance. The importance of the last two depends on the organization. The five roles are:

1. Salesperson

2. Marketeer

3. Organization Observer

4. Counselor

5. Coach

This is your primary role

SALESPERSON:
There is an old sales training axiom that says "nothing happens until somebody sells something." This is true whether you're selling cars, cosmetics, or placing a job applicant with an employer. As a job developer, your job is to seek out potential employers, determine their needs, match employer needs with client needs and, finally, convince the potential employer to hire your client. This is your goal and the ultimate measure of your effectiveness. Thus, the role of salesperson is your primary role.

Selling requires persuasiveness, persistence and resilience. No one likes to be sold or conned, but they don't mind being persuaded. If you can show an employer the benefits to be gained by hiring your client, you'll make a sale, but here's where the second attribute comes in. Few sales are made on

Keep trying

the first call; most take two, three or more calls. Without persistence, you can become discouraged, demotivated and finally, just give up. Don't fall victim to discouragement. Strive to keep yourself and your fellow workers in an "up" mood.

The third attribute is resilience. Anyone involved with selling must learn to deal with rejection. It's a normal part of the job. The key to dealing with sales rejection is to recognize that it's usually not personal. Your proposal is being rejected because the customer can't see the benefit to himself, or else he has received a better offer from a competitor. If your proposal is rejected, step back and analyze the situation, and try it again.

Stay positive

Successful selling also requires a proper frame of mind and a positive attitude. This attitude must be based on self-confidence and a belief that you can do your job and do it better than your competitors. Of particular importance to your success as a job developer is a basic empathy toward the employer rather than toward the client. Those agencies who have been most successful in building a large employer population, have reported this employer orientation to be the key to their success.

Be employer-oriented

To sell effectively, the salesperson must have a good knowledge of selling skills, customer needs, and his product. For you this means an understanding of selling techniques used in selling services. It also means that you understand the employers basic business and, finally, that you know your own agency and the clients you're placing. Since retention, your long-term success factor, is dependent on a good employer-client match, it's important to understand that knowledge of both your employer and client is essential.

MARKETEER:
Marketing is defined as those pre-sale activities designed to help a sales force to maximize their sales efforts. The marketing function was estab-

3

Use a planned approach

lished when it was recognized that a planned, orderly approach to selling a product produced better results. The basic marketing functions include:

● Market research — identifying the customer and his needs.

● Market planning — establishing an overall plan of action for selling a product.

● Advertising — making the product known to the customer population.

● Customer relations — determining customer reaction to, and satisfaction with the product.

Job developers seldom enjoy the luxury of having someone market the agency's services for them. This puts the burden for marketing on you. Therefore, as a marketer of your services, you need to do the following:

● Identify the kinds and numbers of potential employers in your geographical area,

● Understand local business conditions,

● Advertise or in some way make known the existence and purpose of your agency,

● Develop a marketing strategy and plan that will increase your placement rate.

Creativity is essential

A key attribute of a successful marketeer is creativity. Since most agencies operate on limited budgets, the most challenging aspect of your marketing effort will be the creative use of these limited funds.

Accompanying this attribute of creativity should be an attitude of superior service. You must believe and be able to prove that the service you provide is superior to your competitors. Finally, the knowledge required to be a successful marketeer includes a basic understanding of marketing techniques, your job market and your competitors. It is also helpful to know what local agencies and organizations can supply you with marketing support and assistance.

In summary, a well planned and executed marketing effort goes a long way toward making your sales efforts successful. The time spent on marketing will pay off when you're out selling.

ORGANIZATION OBSERVER:
The long-term success of your placement efforts will be determined ultimately by your retention record. While skill in selling and marketing is important to making the initial placement, long-term retention will depend largely on making a good employer-client match. Client-employer matchmaking requires that you be a good organization observer. This means visiting an employer and being able to diagnose the existing work environment for the methods used in handling employee problems, the work rules, regulations and expected behaviors and anything else required of the employees. As an organization observer, your objective is to get an accurate "reading" of the employer and his organization. This takes good perception and an inquiring mind. Techniques used in organization "reading" include:

"Read" employer needs

● Interviewing the employer to determine what he expects of his employees.

● Visiting the work location to observe the physical and psychological working conditions.

● Talking to other employees to get their perception of the employer's expectations and working conditions.

Remember that your role is to describe the environment, not to judge or criticize the organization. An environment that you feel is unsuitable for you may

5

be a perfect match for someone else. The most important element in being effective as an organization observer is your knowledge and understanding of business organizations and jobs within your local area.

For example: If you're familiar with manufacturing assembly operation, you'll be able to assess an employer and his work environment far better than if you have never seen assembly type work. If, on the other hand, you're inexperienced in the kinds of industries operating in your area, take some time to visit them and tour the plant or department. Most employers will be happy to help you. But, however you do it, learn all you can about business organizations and their operations so that you can make good client-employer matches.

The roles of salesperson, marketeer, and organization observer are obviously your major roles, since they are tied directly to the placement effort. The last two roles, counselor and coach, are frequently overlooked or considered to be the province of members assigned specifically to these activities. However, as a job developer working closely with both the client and the employer, you have an excellent opportunity to act also as counselor and coach, and, thereby, increase the effectiveness of your placement activities.

Counselors advise

Before we discuss the specifics of each role, let's be certain we understand the difference between the two. A counselor provides personal advice and assistance dealing with individual behaviors and attitudes, usually based on a personal value system. A coach, on the other hand, serves more as a teacher of skills. For example, counseling involves helping an individual to understand what basic work behaviors and attitudes are expected by an employer, such as, why they are expected to get to work every day on time. A coach assists a client to become more proficient in specific tasks or skills, such as job interviewing or completing a job appli-

Coaches teach

6

cation. Perhaps the easiest way to understand the difference is to say that a counselor helps a person with his thinking, a coach helps a person with his doing— counseling involves values and judgement; coaching involves skills and physical capabilities.

COUNSELOR:

While most agencies use trained counselors in the job readiness phase, successful agencies recognize the wisdom of using job developers in a counseling role during and after the placement phase. Whereas the specifically designated counselor can help the client gain a general understanding of what will be expected of him in the work environment,

Be a counselor to employer and client

your knowledge of the employer and the real world of work in your area makes you an important part of both pre- and post-placement counseling efforts. There is also an opportunity to serve as counselor to the employer helping him to understand some of the problems of the economically disadvantaged. But whether or not a clearly defined counselor role is identified for you, every job developer should be aware of the need to serve in this capacity and recognize the opportunities when they occur.

COACH:

As described earlier, coaching is synonymous with teaching. As a job developer you will have many opportunities to serve as a coach. These opportunities will occur daily while you are working with both the client and the employer.

While working with the client, you will have opportunities to coach the individual in job finding techniques, job interviewing skills and even in specific work behaviors.

Coach in supervisory techniques

If this is an employer's first experience with your agency, you can increase the possibility of it being a positive experience by coaching him in what to expect and how best to supervise your client. Some employers are unaware of biases and stereotypes communicated verbally or nonverbally. A client may be offended by an employer saying, "Hey kid, take this part down to the shop." While the use of the word "kid" was not intended to be a put-down, the client may have perceived it to be so. Coaching the employer to use the new employee's first name will help to avoid these possible problems.

Successful coaches have two things in common; they are excellent observers and good diagnosticians. By observing the actions and behaviors of an individual, they can diagnose areas needing improvement and provide help in making those improvements. Coaching requires an attitude and belief that people want to learn, want to improve, providing they understand the benefit that improvement can bring. It also requires that you believe people will learn and improve with your help and encouragement.

Learn to question, listen, observe, demonstrate

Certain skills and knowledge are required to be an effective coach. These include skills in questioning, listening, observing and demonstrating. By asking questions and listening to the answers, a coach can determine whether the person being coached understands the subject matter. Likewise, by observing the individual perform or behave, the coach can determine the level at which the person can perform the skill required. Based on these answers and observations, the coach can then diagnose the individual training needs for improvement.

The last skill required for an effective coach is the ability to demonstrate the skill or behavior required. Demonstration visually instructs the person being taught in a way that is easy to understand and follow. It is the most effective coaching technique. Keep in mind, also, that your behavior while working with the client serves as a role model that can influence the client in a positive or negative way.

Summary

To describe the position of a job developer in terms of duties and responsibilities alone is inadequate and incomplete. The job must be described and understood as having many dimensions and roles. An understanding of these roles will aid you in working to increase the quality and quantity of your placements. Now that the major roles have been identified, assess yourself against these roles to determine which role needs to be strengthened and where you need to place more effort. A self-assessment exercise has been provided at the end of the chapter to help you.

Role Self-Assessment

Using the 5 roles described, assess your own behaviors as a job developer in each of the categories. Identify those roles that you feel are your strengths and those where you tend to need improvement. Indicate each by an S or W.

Salesperson

☐ Job development is selling
☐ I know and use sales techniques
☐ I am persuasive in my sales efforts
☐ I do not get discouraged by rejection
☐ I am persistant in my sales efforts
☐ I am competitive

Marketeer

☐ I have systematically identified my potential employer population
☐ I am aware of local business conditions
☐ I use all the advertising methods available to me
☐ I have a marketing strategy

Organization Observer

☐ I frequently visit employers to become familiar with their operation
☐ I am familiar with the kinds of industry in my area and their requirements
☐ I understand the working environments of my employers
☐ I make every effort to match the working environment of the employer with the personality of the client

Counselor

☐ I fully recognize and accept my role as a counselor
☐ I provide information to my client and others in my agency about employers
☐ I am involved with post-placement counseling
☐ I counsel the employer during the early stages of the placement

Coach

☐ I recognize my role as coach
☐ I coach clients on the interview process
☐ I serve as a model for my clients

Roles that I want to strengthen:

Develop a specific plan for each role you wish to improve:

2

When the Real World
Isn't The Ideal World

Overview

The world of the job developer consists of an agency, the client and the employer. If you could control all the variables operating in this environment, there's a good chance you would enjoy a high degree of success. But complete control of one's environment is only attainable in the ideal world. In the real world only limited control is possible.

In this chapter we will examine the major factors encountered in your work. They are divided into three groups: 1) those you cannot control, 2) those you can possibly control, and 3) those you can control. This breakdown is intended to help you focus your attention on those controllable factors that will help you to attain the highest possible level of success.

The World of the Job Developer

To the uninitiated, job development would seem to be a simple, straightforward process. First, find an employer with a job opening. Next, identify a job applicant with the required skills. And finally, bring both together to determine if there is a fit. But anyone who has worked as a job developer would be quick to point out that this is an oversimplification of a complex process.

As a job developer your time is spent working with the agency, the client and the employer. The interactions of these three groups creates a complex and variable environment. These variables can be as broad as the general health of the economy, and as narrow as the relationship between a particular job developer and an individual personnel director within a company. Your success in making a good placement is tied closely to your ability to recognize and deal with these variables.

**Classify
the variables**

The following pages contain a description of a general model, Figure 1, designed to guide your thinking and approach to dealing with these variables. They are classified according to the degree of control or influence you have over them as follows:

● Those that you cannot control

● Those that you may potentially control

● Those that you can control.

Those variables that you cannot control tend to have a restraining effect on your overall effectiveness, while those that you can control have the potential to increase your effectiveness. By knowing which variables fall in which categories, you can then focus your efforts on those that will help you most.

Factors That Cannot be Controlled

With few exceptions, the factors beyond the control of the job developer are also beyond the control of the agency. The major factors in this category include:

● Labor market conditions

● Presence of competing placement agencies

● Staff and material resources

● Characteristics of the clients

● External environment

Save your energy

Generally, these factors cannot be changed or altered by either the job developer or the agency. Therefore, little effort should be made to change them. Any energy previously spent trying to change these factors should be diverted to other, more productive, areas.

Let's examine more closely the factors and the various items that make up each one.

Labor Market Conditions

This factor includes variables such as the location and size of the geographic area being serviced, the number and types of employers in the area, and their locations. It also includes the types of industries and the kinds of occupations available along with the demand for certain skills. Local business conditions, seasonal hiring patterns and the general health of the economy are also examples of variables that cannot be controlled.

Competing Placement Agencies

In most areas of the country there is more than one placement agency. This tends to develop a competitive environment between the agencies as they vie for the limited jobs available. While this competition for employers makes the placement job more difficult, it also adds challenge to the job, and in the long run improves the quality of the placements.

Staff and Material Resources

The availability of supporting staff, materials and funds are beyond the control of the job developer. However, the effectiveness of a job developer is not a function of how much or how many resources are available, but rather, how the limited resources are used.

As a job developer you should recognize this and direct your attention to utilizing the allotted resources, rather than worrying about the lack of resources.

Characteristics of the Clients

Since most agencies get their clients through social agency referrals or walk—ins, the job developer has little control over the characteristics of the client. Similar to the availability of staff and material resources, you must work with the clients you are given. Client variations include:

● Education level

● Previous work experience

● Orientation to work

● Skills acquired

● Personality

● Desire for work

● Motivation

External Environment

This last category is the external environment. It includes legal mandates under which the agency and, therefore, the job developer must operate. National incentives, such as targeted job tax credits, stipends and training funds are examples of positive factors which influence placements but are outside the control of the job developer. Availability of local transportation systems and the presence of supporting services within a community also affect your placement success, but cannot be controlled by you in any way. Here again, is the necessity for understanding these external environment factors so as to create strategies for working with them.

For many job developers these uncontrollable factors represent constraints which tend to frustrate and thwart their efforts. However, those who recognize that these factors are beyond their control and develop strategies for working within these constraints tend to be more effective. Examples of such activities would be:

Develop strategies to deal with:

Large area

● The job developer who, faced with a large geographical area, conducted a study of past placements to determine which part of the area had produced the greatest number of placements. Knowing this, he planned his time, and focused his effort on these areas.

Competition

● Finding herself in a service area with a great number of other placement agencies, this job developer competed successfully by stressing the quality and speed of her service. To reduce the negative aspects of competition and to increase the overall success of all agencies in servicing their clients, she developed a cooperative relationship with other agencies through the exchange of information and job orders.

Limited funds

● Faced with limited funds, one job developer sought contributions from local companies for inexpensive advertising brochures and took advantage of free public service advertising on the local radio station to promote the use of his placement service.

Heavy work load

● As the work-load mounted for one group of job developers, they took two actions. First, they sought to streamline their operation by eliminating some of the administrative requirements and by cooperating with one another through the exchange of information and job orders. Secondly, they employed part-time job developers during peak periods. These were usually graduate students or retired people experienced in business.

Transportation

● Local transportation systems have been cited often as inhibitors of job placements. One agency worked to offset this by attempting to match jobs and clients within the same geographical area. In addition, they found that in some cases the alleged transportation problem was not an absence of transportation, but rather the client's lack of knowledge regarding methods of transportation. Therefore, every client sent out on an interview was given clear instructions as to the best way of getting to the employee's location.

See what training matches available job

Given the responsibility of placing participants who are not well prepared for the work world, the successful job developer must work closely with those responsible for job preparation, keeping them informed as to the nature and requirements of the available jobs. By doing this the agency's training efforts can be better directed at skills and attitudes actually needed in the local job market.

In addition, the successful job developer will also keep himself informed about the level of the client being placed so that the jobs being developed will fit the level of the client.

17

Factors Which May Be Influenced

Job developers should be able to tell the difference between those factors that are not controllable and those that are potentially controllable. If you cannot discriminate between the two, there is an excellent chance that you will not be as successful as you could be. The factors that are considered to be potentially controllable are:

Employers:

Change attitudes

● Often attitudes are the result of an experience, hearsay or lack of information. If you can meet with a potential employer and present examples of positive experiences other employers have had, discuss some of his concerns and provide positive information about your program and the client, there is an excellent chance that you will change his thinking about hiring youth.

Address the competition

● Use of competing agencies. While it should not be your aim to promote a competitive battle between agencies, a meeting with an employer could be held to determine whether or not your clients could also be hired. Or, perhaps the employer would find your client population more appropriate to his needs.

Influence wages, working conditions

● Wage rates. Many job developers have been successful in convincing the employer to offer more than minimum wage for certain kinds of work. Others have been effective by counseling the client not to accept the lowest wage when a range is stated.

● Working conditions. Some job developers have provided employers with helpful information about working conditions that are causing high turnover. Employers responding to these suggestions have improved the conditions and thereby reduced the turnover rate.

● Hiring requirements. Here again, job developers have influenced hiring requirements by meeting with employers to educate them about the kind of training being provided the client. In some cases, a better knowledge of the agency's programs and their clients has helped to change or reduce the requirements.

Modify hiring requirements

In each of these cases the job developers have been successful in influencing the employer's thinking by showing the employer how he will benefit from such a change. Unless you can show the employer how he will gain, there is little chance of influencing his thinking.

Labor Market:

● Unemployment rate. As a job developer you have a secondary influence over the unemployment rate. By making good placements, you stand an excellent chance of increasing job retention and thereby, not contributing to the unemployment rate. More positively, if you can influence an employer to up-grade or promote a worker, you will have opened up an entry-level job that can be filled by another of your clients.

Client:

● Use of agency services. While few job developers have the responsibility for finding clients, contin-ued use of an agency's services can be influenced by the job developer and his ability to make good employer-client matches. If a client is satisfied with a job developed by you, there an excellent chance that he will find this a positive experience and return to the agency for another job or up-grading. There is also an excellent chance that he will refer some friends to you.

Satisfied clients will refer others

Whether you decide to make an attempt to control certain of these factors depends on several consid-erations:

● Objectives — Is it within the agency's purposes and plans to control a particular factor?

● Reputation — Is the agency held in sufficient regard, particularly by the employers?

● Extent of Services — Is the program extensive enough to control the factor?

● Motivation — Does the job developer have the desire and drive to control the factor?

Within these limits, successful job developers have made an effort to influence these potentially controllable factors.

Factors Which an Agency Can Control

The quality that distinguishes the successful job developers from those who are unsuccessful is an ability to perceive and work within the limitations of the job. They do this by focusing their efforts on areas of the job which they can control. These are internal factors completely under the control of the job developer, which influence the agency's ability to evaluate its environment accurately, to make decisions and to act strategically. These internal factors — what they are, why they are important, and how they are related to outstanding job development and placement in actual practice — comprise the greater part of this book.

Make these your primary focus

The six internal factors which can be controlled by the job developer are summarized below. They are fully developed in the chapters that follow.

Client Preparation:

Those activities designed to develop and encourage the client's readiness to work.

Working with Employers:

The efforts made by a job developer to build rapport and convince an employer to hire his agency's clients.

Marketing the Agency's Services:

The techniques used to make the agency services known to both potential client and employer and to attract them to use these services.

Developing Job Developers:

The development of the attitudes, knowledge and skills necessary to be a successful job developer.

The Referral Process:

The establishment of an administrative system to effectively process and keep track of all job offers and referrals.

Job Retention and Post-Placement Services:

The services offered by the job developer designed to insure job retention, as well as up-grade his clients.

Summary

Your success as a job developer begins with a clear understanding of your environment and in particular, your ability to distinguish between those factors beyond your control, those that you might be able to influence and those that are completely within your control. By recognizing these three categories, you will be more effective by directing your time and effort toward those things you can influence.

A General
Job Development Agency Model

**Factors agency
cannot control:**

1. Labor market conditions.

2. Presence of competing agencies.

3. Staff and material resources.

4. Characteristics of the clients.

5. External environment.

**Factors agency
can potentially
influence:**

1. Employers.

2. Labor market.

3. Client

**Factors agency
can influence –
Success Factors:**

1. Working with employers.

2. Client preparation.

3. Marketing the agency's services.

4. Developing job developers.

5. The referral process.

6. Job retention and post-placement services.

Figure 1.

Client Services — Whose Responsibility?

Overview

Client development services, which range from orientation and counseling to education and job skills training, should have one basic purpose — to increase the client's chances for getting and keeping a job. Generally, these services are the element that distinguishes CETA-sponsored employment and training programs from commercial placement services.

In this chapter we will explore these services and ways they work best. Since the job developer's role in providing client services varies among agencies, we'll allow you to decide what you can do within the structure of your own agency, to enhance the effort.

Job Preparation - Who Needs It?

Every salesperson knows that ultimately he or she is no better than the product being sold. If your agency's potential employees are not prepared to function in a job environment, neither you nor your agency has anything of value to offer an employer. If the main purpose of your agency is to place people in unsubsidized, private-sector jobs, then every service should reflect this purpose. After all, an employer cannot be expected to hire your clients unless they are qualified for the job. It is your input regarding what employers are looking for that can determine whether or not the job preparation effort will enhance your agency's placement success.

Key Job Preparation Services

The following list of services outlines the major programs offered by successful agencies. They will, of course, vary according to specific contracts.

Orientation:

There are two basic types — to the program itself and to the world of work. You can help to define the real work world.

Counseling:

This may be in the form of individual or group counseling, as well as career and personal guidance. You can help to pinpoint where today's career opportunities exist and what employers expect from their employees.

Coaching:

The job coach aids the client's transition to work by providing various types of support, follow-up and crisis intervention. Can you interface with the employer?

Education Services:

This service may be basic, remedial, or vocational. What is the minimum level of training needed to get the client into the workplace?

Skill Training:

Skill training may be institutional or on-the-job. Training must certainly prepare clients for demand occupations. What are they in your location?

Supportive Services:

These services may include transportation, health, and family services, or legal and financial aid. The agency may develop referral relationships with local community agencies that provide these services, or the agency may provide some of the services directly.

Job Development and Placement Services

Because these services require on-going contact with employers, your information about employer needs and contacts can be of major importance. Examples include:

Labor market

a. Labor-market information: Clients may be provided with occupational information in the community.

Work experience

b. Work experience: A trial-run job experience to familiarize the client with a job environment.

Public service employment

c. Public-service employment: A subsidized job in a public or non-profit agency, which may lead to a permanent job with that agency.

Job search training

d. Job search training: A service to train clients in securing their own jobs.

To Make It Work – Customize

All agencies offer a variety of services designed to help the client get and hold a job. However, some agencies make the decision that all potential employees will receive all of the agency's services, while other agencies decide that each client will receive services based on "where he or she is today in job development or awareness, and what he or she needs." The first type of agency is most concerned with similarities among clients, the second, with differences among them. The latter agency tends to customize services. This isn't necessarily the easiest way because it requires a more thoughtful assessment and planning process, but it is the most beneficial and rewarding in the long run.

Customizing Begins with Assessment

Test and interview

Ordinarily the assessment process involves testing and interviews with the client and considers job-related factors such as education achievement, work history, and occupation preference, as well as basic language facility, health, legal barriers and environmental considerations like child care and transportation needs.

Developing A Plan of Service

Increase client's employability— quickly

The assessment information provides a basis for constructing a plan of service (often called a Employability Development Plan) which addresses the client's strengths and weaknesses. The primary focus of all services should be to increase the client's employability in the shortest amount of time. Flexibility in structuring the service plan is essential. Ideally there should be several service plan options that vary according to an individual's needs. For those ready for immediate placement, one plan could lead directly to placement services, for example:

1. General Agency Orientation

2. Job Placement

Another service plan could lead to counseling for those who are unclear about their occupation goals and personal abilities, for example:

1. General Agency Orientation

2. Career Guidance Counseling

3. Skill Training

4. Job Placement

For those who are less than job ready and require a more extensive range of developmental services, another plan could provide more intensive services, for example:

1. General Agency Orientation

2. Career and Personal Guidance

3. Health Service

4. Remedial Education

5. World of Work Orientaion

6. Job Placement

You can play a major role in developing service plans that will produce job-ready individuals in the shortest time. Because you have the major contact with the employers, your input regarding neded job skills and attitudes is most important. Your information up-dates, based on the employers' changing needs, can keep your agency producing clients who will be of real value to the business community.

Make It a Joint Effort

Client involvement is essential

Getting the clients actively involved in developing their own plans is highly recommended. Clients can benefit by having a say over decisions that affect their lives. Since many individuals suffer from an inability to make choices, taking an active part in creating their own development plan can be an invaluable learning experience.

This involvement also helps them to be realistic. Many people know the kind of future they want, but their aspirations are not realistic. Preparing a plan first requires that goals be identified. After that, objectives and specific activities leading toward the achievement of those goals must be specified. Thus, plan preparation requires that the client vividly confront present circumstances and future prospects resulting in more realistic goals.

Encourage Them to Take Charge

This encouragement is one of the best ways to motivate your clients and help them feel responsible for their activities. You'll find many opportunities to do it, and here are some tips:

What is the real problem?

a. Look for the real reason behind negative behavior. Do clients really lack the drive and motivation to get a job or do they feel depressed about their own chances of succeeding? There are two very different emotions which should be handled for what they really represent. For example, if you think the client has goals, but lacks confidence in his ability to achieve them, you should give support and encouragement whenever possible.

b. Get clients involved in and allow them to

28

**Allow clients
to make decisions**

have influence over agency decisions and actions which affect them. It is ironic that many agencies who lament the overdependence of clients unknowingly help create this reaction. If clients appear to lack a sense of responsibility, look at your agency's structure. Does it allow and encourage them to be responsible for their actions? Some agencies believe they are doing their job best by doing everything for the client, when, in fact, they are being authoritarian and damaging to their sense of adequacy.

**Hold them
accountable**

c. Clients should be held accountable for carrying out specified responsibilities. Many clients who understand that their individual actions directly affect their lives benefit from their involvement with the agency, whether or not they find a job. Creating this learning atmosphere requires that they be given individual responsibilities which they must carry out.

The underlying theme should be, "This is what we will do to help you, and this is what you will have to do to help yourself." Some suggestions along these lines include coming to interviews on time, bringing required information, maintaining regular attendance, doing homework, studying, calling in when delayed, and so on.

**Hold up
a mirror**

d. Always help clients to understand the consequences of their actions. Part of the "failure syndrome" can be seen in the client who repeatedly acts in a way that is harmful. One way to tackle this is with group counseling sessions among clients. They are often more frank and penetrating in their comments with each other than with agency personnel. These group sessions can be extremely helpful in pointing out to clients that their actions can unfavorably affect others.

29

**No excuses
allowed**

e. Be sympathetic, but also realistic. This applies to everyone in the agency who has contact with the client. Urge them to concentrate on future opportunities and not to dwell on past problems. Discuss goals and responsibilities frequently, keeping in mind the need for understanding the obstacles to achieving these goals without accepting excuses for not making the attempt.

Use The Plan as a Roadmap

Even the most thoughtfully developed service plan should be changeable. Its purpose is to provide structure and direction like a road-map, to the client's use of your agency's services. And, like a road-map, it should be regularly consulted, evaluated, and revised when necessary.

**Review,
revise,
re-direct**

This review should always include the client, and the more opportunities for the job developer to be involved in this evaluation process, the better the system works. You can do a better job of placement when you know the client's capabilities. And you can focus (and redirect, if necessary) the training toward those skills currently needed for specific jobs or for the business community in general.

Job Search Training

Throughout this chapter we have emphasized the importance of client involvement in maximizing the effectiveness of our agency's services. Job developers are becoming more and more aware of the fact that their role goes beyond finding jobs and matching them with qualified individuals. To achieve more lasting results we're learning that it is just as important to encourage our clients to feel responsible for their actions and adopt a "take charge" attitude toward their lives.

**Consider
its possibilities**

Job search training is a client service that has had dramatic results toward these ends. This training should be designed and directed by those who have a good understanding of what employers want and need. Since you, the job developer best fit this description, an overview of successful job search training methods and underlying philosophies is included in this Handbook.

Major Elements of Job Search Training

**Organized in
groups**

1. Clients are organized into groups that stay together for the length of the program — two to three weeks. To obtain the best results, they should be involved on a regular basis and should not be allowed to drop in or out at will.

**Lots of
interaction**

2. Part of the program involves group interaction designed to get everyone talking about their job-hunting experiences, fears, hopes, and plans. Frank, but constructive feedback is emphasized. This helps clients gain a realistic assessment of themselves from other members of the group and to develop a heightened self-image.

Mutual support

3. Throughout the program agency counselors are available to the group members. Other clients may also serve as empathetic counselors. Some programs have clients team up as "buddies," pairs or triads to aid each other in their job search. An important element in all programs is the team sense generated within the group.

**Specific skills
are taught**

4. The learning of specific job skills is vital. Clients learn to use the telephone to contact employers, "sell themselves," handle employer objections, make appointments for job interviews, and to follow up on these leads. In addition, they learn how

to prepare a succinct and attractive resume. Also, they are taught how to prepare initial and follow-up letters, and properly fill out job applications.

Learn to use newspapers and telephone

5. Self-initiated approaches teach clients how to use job search information, how to use newspaper advertisements and commercial phone books to identify prospective employers, and how to contact other information resources, such as past employers, friends, and relatives. Letters of recommendation should be acquired from previous employers, although, at times, this may be difficult.

6. The job search effort is treated like a campaign, utilizing proven marketing techniques. The participant is required to first identify a number of employer prospects and to contact a certain number of them. The use of contact quotas is one of the major secrets to the success of this approach, since the more contacts a job seeker makes, the greater the chances of being hired. To motivate the job seeker to contact employers, their progress in actually talking to employers is monitored, with daily numbers of contacts posted and comparisons drawn between particiapnts.

No limits

7. For a variety of reasons, many job-seekers traditionally restrict their job search to a small handful of advertised opportunities. Therefore, clients are taught to apply for a job even if employers do not currently have openings, since contacts made may lead to information about openings in other companies.

Special Training Techniques

Special training techniques such as role plays and videotapes are very useful. Role playing can be very effective in preparing clients for the job interview. They undergo mock interviews conducted by agency personnel who ask questions similar to

Role plays and video used in training

those an employer may ask. Videotaping the interviews aids in the important process of reviewing and evaluating how well the client did. Clients, agency staff, and other members of the client support group are involved in this review process, and clients practice interviewing until their skills are sharpened and confidence bolstered. Because of the eneptness and fear of most people at being interviewed for a job, the importance of this rehearsal element cannot be overstated.

Other Tools for Job Search Training

In order to receive incoming calls from employers, the program can set up its own switchboard or answering service. Also, job leads of no value to one group member can be pooled. A bulletin board is a good way to post potential job leads. Similarly, the job development unit of the program can share its job leads with job-searching clients. A resume update service should be made available to the client by the agency, as should any reasonable service that will aid the group in their intensive job search.

You may want to consider using some or all of the Job Search principles based on their relative low cost and high success rate among many populations. By developing the skills to find their own jobs, clients acquire an asset which will be of long-term benefit. Also, the tendency of some clients to return regularly to government agencies for placement assistance may be reduced if they are able to manage by themselves.

Summary

☐ Does your agency provide client development services?

☐ Who is involved in programming? Is there a mechanism for input by job developers?

☐ Is it possible to tailor the program to individual client's needs?

☐ Are clients directly involved in planning their use of agency services? Are there regular progress reviews?

☐ Does everyone in the agency work to encourage personal responsibility and self-sufficiency among clients?

☐ Has Job Search Training been considered?

4

Building Bridges
With Employers

Overview

What is the focus of your role as job developer? Helping people find satisfying, future-oriented work — or helping employers secure a stable productive work force? Of course, its both. And since our profession is service-oriented, we must focus on our customer if we're going to be successful. In our business, the customer is the employer.

This chapter will help you identify and tailor your services to satisfy your employers' major concerns. It will offer tips on maintaining a two-way communication that will allow you to be responsive to their changing needs. You'll also find suggested guide-lines to use for evaluating their satisfaction with you and your agency. All of these will help you build a relationship based on respect for you as a professional, service-oriented job developer.

What are Employers Looking For?

**Saving time,
money,trouble**

Increased profits

A successful job developer tries to provide the services that employers need and want. While an emotional appeal to "help the under-privileged" may be well received by a few employers, most see the value of the job development program in simple terms. Can it save them time, money, and unnecessary problems? Ultimately, can the agency help them increase profits? Generally, the successful agencies do not try to appeal to an employer's conscience, sense of pity, or guilt. Instead they show how their services can help an employer reach profit-oriented business goals. This professional approach is based on the philosophy that the most persuasive employer motivation is grounded in the need to achieve a stable, trouble-free and productive work force, at as low a cost as possible.

The Agency's Key Services

While the services may vary from agency to agency depending on the program and nature of the employer community, some combination of the following are usually of key importance:

1. Pre-screening of applicants. A thorough pre-screening and referral of only those who meet the job requirements reduces the number of applicants an employer must interview. Thus, the agency is absorbing some of the employer's costs, in time and money.

Trained applicants

2. Providing trained applicants. This speaks for itself. However, you should be ready to explain how your agency's training prepares applicants for success in the work world.

Counseling, pre-placement services

3. Counseling and other pre-placement services. Generally, employers believe that job preparation services are helpful and contribute to that all-important positive attitude toward work.

Follow-up services

4. Providing supportive follow-up and technical service. When the employer is aware that you and your agency are ready to stand by for help whenever an applicant is hired they feel more confident in dealing with the unexpected and avoiding problems.

Financial incentives

5. Offering financial incentives. Financial support through subsidized on-the-job training contracts and Targeted Jobs Tax credit may

be of interest to some employers. Find out how these programs work so you can recommend them where appropriate. (The Appendix lists where to write for information on Targeted Jobs Tax Credit.)

Reduced advertising costs

6. Reducing their advertising costs. Using the agency as a referral resource provides another form of financial incentive to the employer. If they are able to get good workers through your agency, their cost of advertising can be reduced.

Customizing Your Services

Find Out What's Important to Them:

Talk to them, by phone, or in person

Tell, and ask

Never assume that simply providing these services will bring job orders to your door. You'll need to talk with employers, both on the telephone and face to face. To introduce the agency's service, job developers often have a standard presentation, designed both to tell and to ask. The "telling" describes your program and how the employer benefits by placing job orders with your agency. The "asking" is necessary to determine what is of particular interest to the employer.

If, as you are telling about one of your agency's services (such as OJT subsidies), you learn the employer isn't interested in this particular service, it should be used as an opportunity to ask something like, "If you were to place orders with us and hire our graduates, what would you like us to pay particular attention to?" Similar probing questions can help you get a clear picture of what the employer wants from the agency, or in its prospective employees. Then it is up to you to direct your presentation in a way that shows how the employer's interests will be satisfied.

Show how your services satisfy the employer's interests

Record the "hot buttons"

It is also important to record these employer "hot buttons" on your employer cards which will allow your agency to keep track of the kinds of services needed by the business community.

Give Credit Where Credit is Due

Employer Recognition:

Say thanks

Never underestimate the power of a thank you. Here are some ideas:

■ A "Company of the Month" Award recognizing the employer who has hired the most clients during the past month.

■ Recognition Dinners honoring employers with outstanding records of hiring and retaining clients.

■ Award Plaques and Certificates of Merit singling out employers and publicizing the agency and its services.

Get Them Involved

Since the employer is a consumer of your services, it makes sense that they should have some influence over what you offer. There are several ways to get their particiation and input suggested below:

Use employers as advisors . . .

1. Employer Advisor Group: A group of representatives from several potential employers advises the agency on developing and providing services. This Group may form subcommittees to specialize in a specific area of interest to both employer and agency, for example:

a. Industrial services committee: A group of employers representing a particular industry, such as banking and finance, heavy manufacturing, and so on, advise the agency on the types of services appropriate to that industry.

b. Job placement committee: Some agencies, like the Rehabilitation Institute of Chicago, establish an employer committee to provide job placement direction and resources for the agency's job placement effort. This committee may provide job leads and business contacts to the agency's job developers.

c. Client services and training committee: An employer group studies and defines the types of jobs that will be opening in the employer community in the foreseeable future. This committee also assists in designing programs to train clients to fill up-coming jobs. The committee may also advise the agency on other types of client services that will help future workers function more effectively when employed.

. . . as trainers . . .

2. Employer Instruction: Some agencies ask employers to provide skill training to their own clients. Others ask employers to train their staff in various aspects of the employer's business.

...as interface

3. Employer Intermediary: Under this approach, a committee composed of several individuals selected by the employers acts as a conduit between the agency and the area employers. Employers operate the program, providing job preparation and placement services to the employer community. For example, CABMS, a sub-

grantee of the Chicago CETA prime sponsor, is a formal employer-intermediary whose principal emphasis is the marketing of OJT contracts to small companies in the Chicago area.

Maintain relationships with employer associations

4. Relationships with Associations: Maintaining active relationships with local employer associations such as the Chamber of Commerce, personnel associations, Rotary, and other voluntary and fraternal associations provides an excellent opportunity to promote the agency and stress the agency's interest in providing effective employer service.

Satisfaction Guaranteed

Your employer bridges will need constant maintenance if they are to support a continuous two-way flow of information and service that is beneficial to both. It is up to you to keep the relationship healthy and make sure everyone is satisfied.

While each agency should develop its own system for evaluating employer/agency satisfaction, the following guidelines are suggested as a base:

1. Evaluate the relationship, and do it regularly. It is surprising how few agencies actually bother to check how well they are doing in the eyes of the employers. When asked, most agencies would state that they are highly regarded. Many would be surprised to learn that neither employers nor clients are overly impressed with the services rendered.

Keep checking

A one-time or occasional evaluation isn't enough. Circumstances, people, and needs change. The agency should regularly ask,

"What is good about this relationship and what is wrong with it? How can it be improved?"

Keep employer involved

2. Involve the employer on a continuing basis. This can be done in several ways:

    a. Every time a job developer makes an employer contact presents an opportunity for monitoring the employer's level of satisfaction.

    b. Spot checks, mailed questionnaires and on-site employer interviews can be used.

    c. Employers can be asked to contact the agency at a specific, agreed-upon time to discuss agency services.

    d. Groups of employers can be invited to discuss and to measure the quality of agency service.

Make use of what you learn

3. Use the evaluation information. Asking questions and getting the employer's reactions are only the first steps. Using the information for improvement is the most important step. Regardless of how the information is gathered — questionnaires, interviews or meetings, the information will be of two types. One will be of a general nature suggesting changes for across-the-board improvements in service, for example, "provide better follow-up on placed clients." The other type will suggest specific changes relating to a particular employer, "the relationship with X Manufacturing Company would be better if the job developer was more familiar with our jobs." Both should be handled in a systematic way that results in agency improvements:

a. Record the improvement suggestions.

b. Devise an improvement plan.

c. Monitor action for improvement.

d. Keep employers informed as to progress.

4. Evaluate the agency's satisfaction with employers. At times it is not the employer but the agency that is dissatisfied with the relationship. For example, if a particular company develops a poor reputation because of their mistreatment of agency referrals, the agency will hesitate to work with that employer. You can work to avoid these frustrations by following these suggestions:

Is the relationship good for your agency?

a. Establish standards qualifying employers with whom you will work. (CABMS* has established fairly rigorous standards which employers must meet to qualify for CABMS's OJT contracts.)

b. Continually monitor compliance with these established standards.

c. If agency satisfaction declines, discuss the situation openly with the employer.

d. Work out a solution before the problem is exaggerated and difficult to resolve.

What About Labor Unions?

Understand their role within your employers

Labor unions are going to be present in many of your employer companies. Therefore, they must be considered part of your customer base. Unfortunately, many job developers have a limited understanding of the purpose, status, power, and intent of unions, and often look upon them as hindering their placement efforts. They are reluctant to become involved with union representatives and may even avoid union firms altogether. This attitude is counterproductive since it unnecessarily limits placement opportunities. A far more productive approach is to become familiar with the individual unions operating within a company, learn what you have to offer based on the union's point of view, and, where appropriate, establish a relationship with appropriate union representatives. Many unions have employment and training liaisons whose role is to develop a cooperative working relationship with local operations such as CETA. Obviously, it is in the best interests of the agency to identify and meet these representatives.

Conclusion

Try this exercise in evaluation:

1. Review your customer base and select an employer with whom your agency has worked reasonably well.

2. Set up a meeting with whomever you regularly work for the purpose of a frank discussion concerning the employer/agency relationship. (Suggestion: invite them to lunch.)

3. This evaluation should give the employer an opportunity to review those areas in which you've provided needed service, as well as those needing improvement. Ask open-ended questions, encourage frankness, and handle it as a fact—finding session.

4. Listen with a third ear — how does the employer perceive your agency, and don't be defensive. The time for changing opinions comes later.

5. When you return to your office, discuss your findings with your manager and work out a plan for using the information. (See page 41, "3. Use the evaluation information.")

5

Marketing Your Agency's Services

Overview

No matter how fine your agency's services, you simply can't expect the world to beat a path to your door. In order to maintain a steady flow of job orders, you have to develop an effective method for telling your story and increasing your employer (customer) base. Deciding "Who To Tell, and How To Tell Them" can be an overwhelming task in an already too-busy day.

This chapter offers suggestions that will help you develop an organized, systematic approach for marketing your services each and every time you contact an employer.

Analyze and Define Your Market

The product of a successful marketing effort is that steady flow of job orders which allows you to provide an on-going level of service and increase our value to the business community.

Evaluate all potential employers

A successful marketing effort begins by conducting a market analysis and defining those employers or employer groups who have the greatest potential for your service. Doing this means taking the entire list of employer possibilities and evaluating it according to several complex factors. Sounds impossible, but if taken in steps, it is manageable.

Work as a Team

The analysis and market definition process works best when organized and conducted by a team of agency staff members led by job developers. An examination of the agency's current employer base should help to define the kinds of relationships that are presently working, as well as the industries and occupations for which your clients are well-suited. This team effort also ensures that the defined market is one that everyone will be comfortable with, and not just one person's personal preference.

Look at your current base

Deciding Who to Tell

The evaluation process begins with a look at the labor market and environment. This should include the cross-section of factors discussed in this category covered in Chapter 2. The following are of major importance:

1. Geographic service area.
   This includes its size, number of employers, and the location of employers. These factors all affect the ability of the agency's staff to serve area employers. The distance job developers and clients have to travel to employers relates directly to the total number of employers which the agency might theoretically serve. Use a large, detailed map and define the geographic limits of the area your agency can reasonably serve.

Use a map

2. Industries, occupations.
   Identification of employer groups with similar hiring needs based on industry or occupation can increase the efficiency of your marketing effort. Are there industry groupings within your geographic service area? How about employers in different industries, but having similar occupations (clerical, maintenance)? Highlight them on the map.

Group employers into categories

46

Narrow It Down

Start with general categories and make lists of the kinds of employers or employer groups that exist in your service area. Now begin to make some decisions based on your agency's capabilities and your clients' qualifications. The evaluators outlined below should enable you to do two things:

1. Help you extract from the total employer market a customer prospect list that has the greatest potential need for your service.

2. Help you identify areas within your agency that, if improved or expanded, could increase your potential market base.

Define your list

Using the following evaluators, define your prospect list:

1. Agency training.
If your agency provides training in particular areas, this can be used as a guide to identifying markets for which your clients are well-suited. There is usually a relationship between the personnel needs of employers and the client training offered by the agency. For example, RCA in New York sees its primary market as employers with clerical/secretarial needs. Thus, there is consistency in their defined market and their clerical training program. On the other hand, if you see that a significant number of employers are interested in hiring people with certain attitudes or skills, perhaps you should consider making this training a part of your service.

2. Agency staff size.
In defining its market, the agency must also consider its own capabilities, including its staff size and abilities. The number of job

developers on the agency's payroll and the staff's ability to reach employers and solicit job orders directly affects the agency's marketing effort. It is common for job developers to concentrate on the largest employers in the area since they usually hire more people. However, many agencies focus on smaller firms who individually may have fewer job orders but who accumulatively may account for the greatest number of job placements in the area. Your current staff size will have an influence on this part of the evaluation.

3. Agency staff experience.
Your market selection can be influenced by the particular abilities of the agency's job developers. For example, if a job developer has experience in steel manufacturing, firms of this type would make up one part of the targeted market. Do you or other staff job developers have experience placing people in a particular industry or occupation?

4. Clients' transportation needs.
This is an important market determinant. The employers you serve must be accessible to your clients. Consult your geographic service area map for both employer and participant proximity to transit systems.

5. Clients' skills.
Your clients' skills and job-readiness should both be considered when selecting the employer market. Will they be able to function in these industries or occupations? This ties into the "Agency training" evaluator.

Pinpoint

Identifying your target employers involves another set of evaluators which are best applied when there is some direct contact. However, they are useful in

Targeting charisteristics:

the analysis phase for defining those characteristics that would make an employer a prime target for your services.

Interest

1. Employer interest in your services.
   If you know employers are interested in the kinds of services your agency offers, for example, pre-screening, world of work or skill training, or OJT programs, you can address your presentations, conversations and general marketing efforts to those specific interests and have a much greater chance of acceptance and positive response.

Attitude

2. Employer attitude.
   Some firms have traditions or policies that make a special effort to hire certain populations, such as youth, ex-offenders, the handicapped, women, or veterans. Locating these employers can give you an inside edge.

Work environment

3. Employer's work environment.
   Does it suit your clients' needs? For example, some agencies have found that smaller employers offer their clients a more sensitive and responsive work environment. In other cases, the employer size is not the determinant, but the ability of the supervisor to relate well with the client.

Opportunity for clients

4. Employer opportunity for promotion and growth.
   Job placement is not the final step. Maintaining a flow of job orders is accomplished by providing satisfaction for both employer and employee. Thus, opportunity for your clients' career and personal growth should be considered when selecting employers.

Determining both primary and secondary markets is essential to conducting an organized marketing

Primary and secondary markets

effort. The primary market is the group of employers likely to produce on-going levels of job orders. The secondary market supplements the primary through periodic, seasonal, temporary or special types of job orders. This definition allows an efficient focusing of agency efforts.

What to Say

Developing your message really shouldn't be difficult since you've already defined your market as it relates to what you have to offer. Telling your story is done by making the link. Whether you develop a written presentation, a desk top presentation, flip chart, flyer, direct mail card or talk to someone on the phone, your objectives should be three-pronged.

Use these three elements as your guideposts:

Show you understand their needs

1. Show that you understand the employers needs and requirements. Some things, like good health and positive work attitude, apply across the board. Other needs are industry or occupation-related. The more you know about an employer's business, the more specific you can be.

Link your service to their need

2. Explain how your agency services and client qualifications can satisfy their needs. Link what you have to offer with their need to save time, money and unnecessary problems. (Refer to "What Are Employers Looking For?" in Chapter 4.)

Provide action step

3. Remember that all marketing efforts should encourage and lead to the employer's use of your services. Examples: Postage-paid reply cards and your telephone number on everything printed.

How To Tell Them

**Use a combination
of promotional and
personal contacts**

There are any number of ways. They fall into two categories — promotional and direct personal contact, both of which should be thought through and planned within the entire marketing effort.

It is extremely effective to coordinate promotional items and personal contact. For example, Job for Youth (JFY) in New York emphasizes direct mail advertising coordinated with direct personal contact. Primary market employers are identified, mailing lists purchased, promotional materials prepared and mailed. Follow-up consists of a telephone contact with company representatives. Appointments are made to visit the employer or job orders are solicited directly over the telephone. In addition, JFY also places advertisements in trade papers.

RCA has met with success in its use of job fairs, and has written a song to promote their services. SAFER promotes considerable media coverage, publishes newsletters, and hosts well-publicized awards dinners which draw political, social, and employer leaders in the Chicago area.

The following list represents marketing tools, devices, and techniques currently being used:

Advertising

Telephone book yellow pages
Newspapers
Journals
Area Service Directory
Specialty advertising:
  bumper stickers
  matches
  pens, pencils
  calendars, novelty items
Posters, billboards
Bus advertising
Brochures — hand delivered

Flyers
Quantities of brochures left
in businesses (banks, Post Office)

Special P.R.

News releases
Radio, T.V. announcements
Public service announcements
Talk shows, panels

Employer Mailings

Published participant profiles
Newsletters
Personal letters from staff
Mass mailings
Periodic mailings to inactive employers
Greeting cards

Employer Credit

Award dinners, luncheons, breakfasts

Employer/Participant Involvement

Organizing employer groups to promote
agency among other employers
Testimonials
Referrals

Organized Presentations

Employer Open Houses
Job Fairs
Employer groups, Association
presentations

Track responses

At the end of this chapter are examples of some of these items. Whatever technique is used, it is advisable to monitor and store the information on the responses per technique. For example, when employers contact the agency they can be asked how they learned about the agency. This gives the agency one yardstick for evaluating the cost and effectiveness of each technique.

Even with the cleverest of promotional techniques, the key to successful marketing of your services is direct personal contact. This contact brings the agency to life in the minds of employers. To the employer, the agency is the person who makes the contact. Generally, if they believe the job developer is competent, reliable, and helpful, these positive attributes will be ascribed to the agency as well.

The concept of personalized relationships is an important one. When employers are asked what they are interested in receiving from employment services, private or public, they often request a more personalized service. Employers like having one person whom they can contact, a person who knows and understands their situation and is concerned about providing needed assistance. This desire has resulted in the development by the U.S. Job Service of the Account Executive Program. Under this program, individual staff members are assigned selected major accounts to whom they provide a comprehensive, rapid, and "one-stop" service.

Agencies who receive most of their job orders as a result of personal contacts may not use many promotional activities. JFY in New York and the East Harlem Youth Employment program have both found that developing intensive service relationships requires emphasis on person-to-person contact.

Make phone calls, personal visits

The two principal ways to make personal contact are telephone calls and employer visits. With both, the following are basic to good results:

1. Frequent contact.

2. Skill in telling your agency's story.

3. Agency support and enforcement.

Set personal goals

Many successful agencies have formalized individual goals for personal employer contact with employers with assigned, enforceable quotas. If your agency doesn't have goals of this kind, set your own. Establish a certain number of promotional telephone calls and employer visits to make each day or week.

About Those Field Visits:

Visit employers annually

You should devise a plan for visiting every employer once a year. It generally works well to devote one day or part of a day each week to your field visits. Minimize your travel time by visiting employers who are fairly near each other; the zip code directory can help with this. Use the face-to-face meeting to not only give the employer a chance to tell you what he needs but as an opportunity to evaluate the people and surroundings from your client's point of view.

Screen unsuitable employers

If the employer is not suitable for the kind of clients your agency places, note the reason on an employer card and set it aside for several months or a year. You can contact them sometime in the future to see if either of your situations have changed. This "retiring" of employer name should also occur if you receive no job orders after contacting them regularly for a year.

Using Employer Influence

Don't underestimate the value of your satisfied customer. Ask for referrals and introductions to other employers. An example of using employer influence is a simple process called the Multiplier, used by the Chicago Jobs Now project. The underlying hypothesis is that employers can be influenced to sell the program to other employers. A simple process is followed:

**The Multiplier
Process**

1. A target industry is identified based on size, growth, wages, benefits, and the industry's potential interest in working with the agency.

2. One or two particularly influential employers are contacted and asked to serve as hosts and sponsors for a presentation to other major firms within the industry.

3. A seminar is conducted to promote the use of agency services among the firms in that industry.

4. Job developers, assigned to serve employers on the basis of type of industry, follow-up by personally contacting seminar participants.

Telling your story to two or twenty takes the same amount of your time. Some agencies have successfully expanded their audience by using employer groups and associations as the Chamber of Commerce and Rotary.

The Rehabilitation Institute of Chicago (RIC), for example, works intensively with the Rotary Club of America. Originally, their involvement was limited to provisional recreational and financial support to the Children's Unit, but success and good relations led to the Rotary's interest in doing more. Through RIC's provision of consultation and assistance in the area of handicapped employment, there developed a sizeable concern with the broader vocational needs of the handicapped. At present, RIC works intensively with the Rotary throughout the Chicago area. The impact of this approach has exceeded the highest hopes of RIC. More job orders are forthcoming through the Rotary than RIC can fill. To continue to build on the extraordinary interest generated among Rotary employers, RIC helped to establish links with the Illinois Division of Vocational Rehabilitation (DVR). Service connections were made between DVR offices throughout the state and Rotary locals in the respective communities. The result of this evolving enterprise has been significantly increased employment opportunities for severely handicapped people through a partnership between service club, a rehabilitation facility, and a state agency.

Follow–Up

The on-going nature of the job development process illustrates the importance of good follow-up activity. Follow-up means both following through on something you have promised, and, recognizing the progressive nature of your activities, regularly following one with the next.

Examples:

Promotional mailings ◊ Appointment to explain agency service

Awards dinner ◊ Request for referral to other employers

Supportive service to placed employee	◊ Phone calls or visits to employer to insure satisfaction	◊ More job orders

Summary

Marketing your agency's services is an on-going developmental process. As the economy changes, employer needs change. Since there is a direct relationship between employer needs and agency services, there must be a frequent re-evaluation of the relationship. Take a few minutes now to think about the marketing functions discussed in this chapter, as they apply to your agency.

☐ **Market Analysis & Identification**

☐ **Developing Your Message**

☐ **Reaching Your Audience**

- ● Promotions
- ● Personal Contact
- ● Employer Influence

☐ **Follow-Up Activities**

Attention Employers:
Fill your entry-level jobs
with well-screened, responsible
young adults, 16-21
through

JOBS FOR YOUTH

A NO-FEE EMPLOYMENT SERVICE

Call:
742-5520
119 Charles Street
Boston, Ma. 02114

~ REFERENCE METRIC CARD ~
APPROXIMATE

YOU KNOW:	YOU CAN FIND:	IF YOU MULT. BY:	VICE VERSA BY:
(IN)	MILLIMETERS (MM)	25	
	CENTIMETERS (CM)		0.04
	METERS (M)	30	.033
	KILOMETERS (KM)	0.9	
(IN2)	SQUARE CENTIMET. (CM2)	1.6	1.1
(FT2)	SQUARE METERS (M2)	6.5	0.6
	KILOGRAMS (KG.)	0.09	0.16
	TONNES (T)	0.45	11
	LITERS (L)	0.9	2.2
		3.8	1.1
			0.26
°F	DEGREES CELSIUS (°C)	-32 & 5/9	9/5 + 32

JOBS
YOUTH   742-5520
No Fee Employment Service

If you're ready to get off the street and on the job THE WORLD OF WORK PROGRAM is for you.

What does the World of Work Program do?

Our job is to turn unemployed inner-city teenagers into successful members of the work force. We help teenagers who want to land decent jobs and keep them. We want you off the streets and on the job. We also have a special program called the Hispanic World of Work for Spanish speaking teenagers.

What will I learn?

You will start by learning how to fill out a job application. You will learn how to handle yourself in a job interview. When you know how to answer questions in an interview, you have a lot better chance of landing the job that you want. You will learn how to solve problems that face you once you are on the job. You will learn how to move ahead, how to get a raise and how to gain respect from your boss. You will learn all the things that will help you to find a good job and keep it.

Will the World of Work Program really get me a job?

Yes. We will help you to get a full or part-time job or we will help you to get into a skill training program. If you want to get into college and need help getting a scholarship, we will help you do that too. We will help you with all of the problems that keep you from having a successful working life. Once you are on the job, we will keep in touch with you and your employer on a regular basis so that if any problems come up we will be around to find a solution.

How do I get into this Program?

You must be at least 16 years old but under 20 years of age and come from a low income family. You have got to prove to us that you really want to join this program. If you call us and talk to one of our staff members, we will help you in any way that we can.

What do I do once I join?

You must attend the group training sessions for one month. You must try to do your absolute best, attend every class and be there on time. You must take part in group discussions and prove to us that you deserve a job by giving us your best.

Can I really land a job through World of Work?

This program has connections to Boston's major hospitals, banks, restaurants and retail establishments. This program has proved that it can produce successful workers with good work habits so that when we make a phone call for you your chances of getting a job are good. We have placed our enrollees as sales clerks, waiters, cashiers, nurses aids, file clerks, recreation workers, laborers, printer trainees, and in many other types of positions.

What about special problems?

We can handle any problem that you encounter; and if we can't handle it ourselves, we will refer you to the best possible source of help.

What is the special program for Spanish speaking teenagers?

The Hispanic World of Work Program prepares 16 to 18-year old teenagers for a successful job experience. The program includes communication skills, interviewing techniques and many other topics you need to compete successfully. Once you complete two months of group sessions, you work on a one-to-one basis with a job developer who sets up an interview for you in private business. Once you are placed on a job, we will keep in contact with you in order to help you through any problems that might arise.

6

Job Development is Really Selling

Overview

Job developers are story-tellers, matchmakers and dream-builders, all rolled into one. In actuality, the requirements of your job make it a selling process, from start to finish. The process for selling anything, product or service, can be defined using a step-by-step approach. Whether your communications with a potential employer are written or verbal, they will be most effective if you consider and use these steps when planning and presenting your message.

This chapter outlines The Ten Essentials of Selling and offers suggestions for applying them to your activities. The intent is to introduce you to a structured approach to selling used by successful salespersons. It is not, however, a complete course in selling. As a guide to further personal development, a list of attitudes and abilities possessed by successful job developers is also included.

Job Development is Selling

Responding to the question "What does it take to be a successful job developer?", an individual with many years of social service experience answered this way: "When I first became a job developer someone told me that it was a sales job. I was repulsed by the idea. It conjured up an image of a slave block...I wanted no part of that. After my first few weeks on the job, I began to understand what they meant. I learned that success in job development was tied directly to my ability to sell, to convince an employer that my client could do a job for him. Once I realized this, I then recognized the fact that I had better learn something about selling."

Job development is, indeed, selling. And while some novice job developers have some difficulty accepting this initially, most come to recognize the validity of this statement after a short time on the job.

Let's examine what is required to fulfill this salesperson role. A salesperson is responsible for getting a potential customer to buy or accept his or her product or idea. While the specific approach to selling a computer may be different from getting a job order, the basic process of selling is the same.

The Ten Essentials of Selling

The process of selling consists of ten essential steps organized in three phases:

I Pre-sale preparation	3 steps
II Making the Sales Call	5 steps
III Post call evaluation and follow-up	2 steps

I PRE-SALE PREPARATION:

Whether you are making a call on a previously identified potential employer or just canvassing an area, pre-sale preparation is important. This preparation should include, as a minimum:

Step 1 Identify your prospective "buyer":

● What company do you plan to call on?

● To whom do you want to talk?

● What do you know about the company, i.e. size, location, industry, kind of work?

● What are their employment needs?

● Have they used your service before? was it successful?

Step 2 Establish call objectives:

● What do you want to happen as a result of your call?

● What approach are you going to take?

● What do you have to offer?

Step 3 Plan the meeting:

● Select a convenient time and place

● Call ahead for an appointment

● Be on time

● Don't take too much time, but also, don't rush.

Pre-sale preparation is important; don't overlook it. By being prepared, you can anticipate questions and objections and thereby, increase your chances of getting an order or achieving whatever call objective you had established.

II MAKING THE SALES CALL:

The next five steps make up the traditional approach to any sales call:

● Getting attention.

● Identifying the customer's needs.

● Presenting a solution to satisfy the need.

● Selling the value of your solution.

● Getting commitment or action to accept your solution.

Let's look at each step more closely.

State a benefit and ask a question

Step 4 Getting attention: The first objective when calling on an employer is to get his attention by telling him who you are and why you are there. This means describing your agency and the service you provide. It should be done quickly and in such a way as to get the employer's attention, for example: "Good morning, I'm George Howard from the Intercity Foundation. For the past two years we have been serving local employers by finding capable employees to fill their entry level jobs. Are you familiar with our service?"

Get the employer talking

This question gets the employer talking and, depending on the response, gives you your next move. Of course, if you've done your pre-call preparation properly, you'll know the answer to the employer's comments or answer. If the answer is "no", describe your agency and its service. If the answer is "yes", ask how he heard of it and whether or not he has used the service. Remember, your purpose is to get their attention and start to establish rapport.

Be ready to answer objections

In any call situation you must expect and be prepared to handle objection. The following represents some typical objections and possible responses you could use:

OBJECTION	RESPONSE
I don't have time to talk now...	I'd like to make an appointment to tell you how we can help you...
I had a bad experience with an agency like yours...	I'm sorry to hear that. Can you tell me more about the problem and we can discuss what we would do to prevent that from happening again...

| I don't have any need right now.. | Why don't I take a few minutes to tell you what we can do for you, then, when you have a need, you can call us. |
| I'm already using another agency's services... | I'm glad to hear that. Who are you using... perhaps our service could complement your present service. |

Being adept at answering objections takes time. Try to anticipate all the possible objections a potential employer could have and develop responses to them. Talk with an experienced job developer and find out how he or she handles objections. However you do it, you must learn how to deal with objections.

Step 5 Identifying the need: Unless a potential customer recognizes a need for your product, there is little chance of making a sale. As a job developer this means identifying potential employers who seek to hire employees similar to the type of clients you serve. For example, employers with a high turnover rate on entry level jobs, are excellent candidates for your service. Be aware that in some cases the employer may not realize the need. This means **Ask more questions** that you must help the employer to recognize that need. Certain questions can be used to draw out the employer to determine his needs and, at the same time, help him to recognize these needs, for example:

● Are you experiencing high turnover in your entry level jobs?

● Does high turnover create problems and cost you money?

● Do you have problems filling these jobs?

These kinds of questions are directive questions. You use them to get a "yes" answer in order to get the employer to recognize his need. These questions or ones like them, would be followed by non-directive questions designed to get the employer to talk more about the problem.

● How do you go about getting employees to fill these openings?

● How much time do you spend trying to find replacements?

● What do you find to be your greatest problem?

After getting the employer to talk about the problem and his specific needs, you are ready to present him with a solution to his problem.

Gain agreement on need

"It would seem that if I could provide you with a supply of potential employees pre-screened and ready for work, that would be valuable to you." When you get agreement on this point, you're ready to go into Step 6.

Suggest a solution

Step 6 Presenting a solution: Your product or service is presented as a solution to the potential buyer's recognized need. As a job developer, your placement service can be the solution to the employer's hiring needs. Solutions should be presented in terms of "features and benefits." Features represent those unique services provided by your agency; benefits are what the employer gains from each feature. A pairing of your features and benefits would look something like this:

Stress benefits

Features — What you provide	Benefits — What the employer gets
pre-screening	background or reference checking not necessary

trained applicants	employees ready to work. No lost time training them.
counseling	employees with the proper orientation to the work world. They know what to expect...they make better employees, retention is improved.
follow-up	agency maintains a relation-ship with both employer and employee to ensure the proper match and counsel employee when necessary.
financial incentives	employer can receive subsidies for on-the- job training, also targeted jobs tax credits are available.
available supply of potential employees	reduces time and money necessary for recruiting and advertising.

Your primary objective in this step is to get the employer to admit that your service is one solution to the problem or need that exists. Your next step is to convince the employer that your solution is the best.

Step 7 Selling the value of your solution: Each employer will view the features and benefits differ-ently. What is of great value to one may be of little value to another. It is your job to present all the fea-tures and benefits of your service and then to deter-mine which are of most importance to the employer. This is called "finding the buyer's hot button."

Find the "hot button" and concentrate on it

Once you have determined that benefit valued most, concentrate your selling efforts primarily on that one. Do not stress features and benefits that the employer does not value.

65

At this point in the selling process you have accomplished the following:

● Gotten the employer to recognize a need for entry level employees.

● Presented your service as a solution to this need.

● Established the value of your service to the employer.

While many salespeople can get a potential customer this far in the selling process, many have difficulty with the next step.

Get the employer's commitment

Step 8 Getting commitment or action to your solution: While the first four steps are important to the selling process, it is this last step which brings your efforts to a positive close. Getting commitment means having the customer sign the order. In your case, this means having the employer give you a job order. Of course, it is not always possible to come away from an employer with a job order, particularly if he doesn't have an opening at that time. In this situation, you should work to get a commitment from the employer to call you as soon as a job is available. It's also a good idea to keep in touch with the employer so that his commitment to you isn't forgotten.

III POST-CALL EVALUATION AND FOLLOW-UP:

After each call, whether you have received an order or not, you should carry out the following:

Evaluate the call

Step 9 Evaluate your call: How well did you follow each step...what did you do best, where were you weakest... what would you do differently next time. Also, ask yourself why you did or didn't get an order. Many highly successful sales organizations use a formal review after each sale or loss. They attribute much of their success to this kind of debriefing.

Step 10 Follow-up: It should be part of your selling effort to follow-up each order to ensure that you delivered what you promised and to determine the customer's level of satisfaction with your service. Remember, future sales, job orders, will come as a result of employer satisfaction. It's up to you to be certain the employer is satisfied. If, however, a call did not result in a sale, periodic follow-up should still be made to remind potential employers of your service. There's always the possibility that you'll get an order on your second try.

Future sales will come from customer satisfaction

Selling Skills

In addition to using the 10-Step approach to selling, two specific skills are required — presentation skills and communications skills.

Presentation skills:

As a salesperson for your agency you will need the ability to make convincing sales presentations to both individuals and groups of employers. A good presentation requires a balance of explanation, questions and responses and will be most effective if well planned and rehearsed.

Plan and rehearse

The job developer who does all the talking without giving the employer an opportunity to speak is doomed. An important way to hold the employer's interest is to involve the employer actively in the presentation, for example, review the agency's brochure, view a presentation aid, or enter information on an agency form. Since employers also become involved in a presentation when they speak, a good job developer will ask questions that require the employer to respond verbally. Questions should be used not only to involve the employer, but to direct the presentation and address employer concerns and needs.

Involve your audience

Communication skills:

Practice using role-play

Skill in questioning, listening and responding goes hand-in-hand with making a good presentation. These skills can be practiced with fellow workers by role playing the developer's and employer's parts in mock sales calls.

The primary purpose of a presentation is Step 8 — getting commitment or action to accept your solution. It is often called "The Close." The most desirable "close" is a job order. Despite the fact that this is the goal of most employer presentations, many developers do not close or make any serious attempt to close.

Concentrate on the close

To improve your ability to close — specifically, to ask the employer for a job order — practice rehearsing a presentation that requires a close.

The Right Frame of Mind

Using The Ten Essentials of Selling and effective presentation and communications techniques will go a long way toward helping a job developer achieve success. There are other factors, however, which must be present to ensure this success. We'll define the other factors as "the right frame of mind."

The job developer's working life style requires certain attitudes and abilities:

Use self-discipline

● Self-discipline — As a job developer you will spend most of your time interacting with others. You will enjoy a great deal of autonomy and independence, which requires a high degree of maturity and self-discipline. Time management and self-organization are essential to your effectiveness.

**Be
physically
active**

● Physical activity — There is a great deal of moving around required to meet individual employers, employer groups, and to securing information outside the office. A person who prefers a calm, slow-paced work role will probably not be fully comfortable as a job developer.

**Learn to
pace yourself**

● Ability to handle constant demands — unlike many jobs, the job developer seldom has a chance to let down. The activities and pressures of the job are constant. There are few rest periods. To ensure that you don't burn out, you must recognize the demanding nature of the job and learn how to pace yourself.

Certain personality traits have been found to contribute to the "right frame of mind" discussed earlier. While there is no guarantee of the success or failure of a job developer based on these traits, there is a high correlation between the presence of the traits and success.

**Develop these
traits:**

persuasiveness

● Persuasiveness — The bulk of the developer's job involves communicating with others to promote a specific concept or service. Although a way with words is certainly helpful, what matters most is your ability to transmit a compelling and persuasive message.

self-confidence

● Social ease — Contrary to common belief, it is not necessary that a job developer be a gregarious and outgoing individual. There are many high-excelling developers who are reserved and mild-mannered. However, as a job developer you should be able to establish rapport with both employers and participants.

**ability to create
good impression**

● Ability to favorably affect others — Whatever your personal style, you should be able to make a favorable impression on others, particularly employers. What impresses employers most (though of course employers vary as markedly as developers) is a combination of friendliness, competency, and reliability.

assertiveness

● Assertiveness, imagination and persistence — Far too many job developers are put off by the employers' first "no." Good developers have learned not to take "no" for an answer. They try again, asserting themselves without alienating the employer, often persisting until they succeed.

enthusiasm

● Commitment and enthusiasm — One has to be impressed with the number of job developers who pass up better paying job opportunities because of their desire to work with and improve the status of the unemployed workers. The good developer handles the job with a contagious enthusiasm which is transmitted to potential employers.

resilience

● Resiliency — As previously stated, you will frequently face disappointment and discouragement. Since most employers contacted by the developer do not agree to work with the agency, developers need to air their frustrations, let off steam, and get back to work.

Conclusion

Job development is selling and selling requires planning and analysis. The exercises below are designed to help you to plan and analyze your sales approach. Use them in preparing for your next and subsequent sales calls.

Pre-sale Preparation

Pre-sale preparation and potential employer record card can be combined. A 3x5 card can be prepared and used for this dual purpose. A sample card is shown on the next page. The pre-sale preparation material can be completed before each call. The reverse side is then used to record notes and information for future follow-up or action.

PRE-SALE PREPARATION

Company Name | Address | Tel. No.

Contact | Title

Industry/Kind of work

Call Objectives:	Sales Approach:

Side 1

POTENTIAL EMPLOYER RECORD

Call Date	Call Summary: Reaction – Potential – Follow-Up Action

Side 2

Sales Call Guide

Use this Guide to establish a structure for your sales calls. It will probably take a few calls before you settle on the one that is most effective for you. The important thing, however, is to establish an approach that is smooth, professional, and gets results.

Sales Call Outline
Getting attention: This includes your greeting, your opening statement and the purpose of your call.

GREETING:

OPENING STATEMENT/ATTENTION GETTER:

PURPOSE OF CALL:

Identifying the Need: Ask a question that will draw out the employer and help to establish the need:

Present a solution: Your solution is your agency's service. Outline the features and benefits of your service.

Features

What you provide.

Benefits

What the employer gets.

Sell the value of your solution: Ask a question that will identify the features and benefits that are of the greatest value to the employer:

The Close: At this point, you should ask a question or make a statement that will get the employer to make a commitment to use your service:

You can also expect to get some objections. Be prepared for these objections by being ready to answer the objections. List the possible objections you have encountered and your answer to them:

OBJECTIONS

YOUR ANSWER

7

Developing a System for Job Development

Overview

The job development process is enormously complicated with detail and requires a good deal of organization if it is to be a successful effort. Developing a systematic approach to securing job orders and matching them with qualified participants is absolutely essential to your effectiveness — and sanity.

This chapter looks at methods used in well-managed job development and referral systems, and offers examples which can be readily adapted to your own activities.

Managing the Job Development Process

Organize your employer list

Your system for managing the job development process begins with developing a method for working with an employer list. How is your employer list defined? To avoid confusion, a consistent method for allocating employers among job developers should be used. Most agencies use the following elements, alone or in some combination:

    a. Alphabetic

    b. Industry or occupation group

    c. Geographic proximity

A consistent allocation system lets you know who you are responsible for, and makes it much easier to establish a regular system for contacting your employer list. Some agencies recommend contact

**Use a
control
mechanism**

every two weeks, by phone or visit. A control mechanism, such as file box and employer cards, is essential. Indexing should separate primary and secondary markets. Within these, further index your employer list in categories that simplify your contact procedure, for example, zip code, size, and occupation. Each category should be alphabetized.

**Record each
contact**

The results of each and every contact must be recorded. Even if you don't get a job order this time around, try to learn more about the firm which will help you on the next contact. Examples are size, location, exact nature of the business, and busy season. These ongoing records will provide a store of information that will allow you to better present yourself and your agency in future calls.

Handling the Job Order

What happens when you do get a job order? While there are various divisions of labor within agencies which affect the taking of job orders, one element is common in all successful agencies. Meticulous attention is given to recording complete, accurate information.

**Carefully
record details**

Remember our objective. With job order in hand, we want to get a qualified client to the employer for an interview— and do it as quickly as possible. An organized, consistent procedure for handling job orders goes a long way toward this end.

**Use a
standard form**

A standardized form helps to make certain everything is covered. Order takers, whether they be job developers, counselors, or other staff, should be trained to ask clarifying questions and summarize the information recorded. Most employers take many of their requirements for granted. Without increasing these by implication, the job developer needs to find out exactly what is wanted.

Examples: "How much schooling should the applicant have?" not "Do you require a High School Graduate?" If experience is required, must it be in the specific area or can it be generalized?

Use this list as a guide:

■ Job description

■ Hours

■ Salary— range or minimum (not "open")

■ Applicant requisites: age, sex, education

■ Employer location (floor), contact

■ Travel directions, transportation access

If the job order is from a new employer you should also send them agency literature, a personal letter, and plan to visit them on your next field visit.

Heading off potential problems:

Many employers see inaccurate job order information as one reason why agencies send unqualified clients. It can also create unnecessary delays in getting them to the initial interview. When there is time, some agencies send a copy of the job order to the employer for confirmation.

Verify job order information

Many agencies report that in most entry-level jobs, employers require credentials that have little actual bearing on the client's ability to carry out the job. Then they tend to underemploy the people they hire. For example, in taking a job order for a messenger clerk, the agency may learn that the employer is seeking a high school graduate with two years' experience. Based upon the agency's experience, these requirements will make the job hard to fill and may result in a high turnover. To increase the chances of placing one of its own

Influence hiring requirements

graduates (and to stabilize the position so the employer does not continually have to fill it), the agency may suggest lowering the requirements of the job.

Ordinarily, the agency does not suggest that a potential employer change its hiring requirements until it has developed a stable, fairly long-term trust relationship with the employer. Once a firm relationship is established, the agency is in a more favorable position to suggest tactfully that the employer's difficulties in hiring and retaining personnel may, in fact, have something to do with the employer's own practices.

Don't attempt the impossible

Some agencies create problems for themselves by taking job orders which are difficult, if not impossible to fill. Some agencies deal with this by accepting the order conditionally after informing the employer that it may not be possible to fill the order. Once aware of the agency's problem, the employer can decide to let the agency try to obtain a job candidate or give the order to another agency.

Keep the employer informed

If you ever expect problems in filling an order, always inform the agency. Few flaws in agency servicing are as disturbing to the employer as not being informed of the actions being taken on job orders. By informing employers of any or all problems in filling an order, you'll generally reduce the chances for employer disappointment. Indeed, the inviolate rule of thumb in servicing all job orders is that the employer should always know the status of the order.

The Job Order Pool

The speedy referral of a qualified participant is of utmost importance and most successful agencies feel this is best accomplished when everyone has full access to all job orders brought into the agency.

**A method for
speedy referral**

Most agencies use some form of centralized job pool. All job orders are routed to a central point and made available to all placement staff.

a. Order pooling in a small agency, for example with two placement individuals, may simply mean that the two people work from the exact same job order form.

b. A slightly larger agency may place all job orders in a tray or box, or may post the orders on a bulletin board.

c. A larger agency may photostat copies of all orders — one copy for each placement staff member.

d. The most sophisticated job pool is a computerized job bank usually located in an urban area with many branch and satellite offices.

**How the
system works**

The method for job pooling at VFI in New York also provides a mechanism for tallying agency activities for their reporting requirements. The job pooling system works as follows:

1. The Job Order Card

   a. Original in Job Order Box (alphabetically)

   b. Copy in Control Book

2. The Board Card
   Condensed information concerning the job order posted on bulletin board, according to job category (clerical, messenger, sales, etc.)

Counselors review job openings posted on bulletin board. If they have a candidate in mind, they initial the Board Card and take the Job Order Card from the box. If the job order is for more than one job, extra copies are made for the Job Order Box and the number of openings noted on the Board Card.

The team approach

At RCA in New York, a job developer and counselor work as a team to fill orders. The teams specialize in certain industries and occupations, developing a good understanding of specific employer needs. They work closely to establish training curricula and prepare their clients for interviews. However, if a job opening exists and the team has no qualified participant to send for the interview, the job order is passed on to another staff team. (Sample VFI and RCA cards are reprinted at the end of this chapter).

This open access to job orders increases your agency's chance of satisfying the needs of both clients and employers. There is never any long-term gain in holding orders out of the pool in anticipation of the "right client coming along." It just deprives other clients of a possible interview, unnecessarily protracts referral time, and creates employer dissatisfaction.

Making the Match

Classify job orders

In most agencies job orders are classified by job type (clerical, shipping clerk, driver, etc.). The codes from The Dictionary of Occupational Titles (DOT) or other standard classification codes are usually used. At some point in the process of working with the clients a similar code is entered on their records. Thus, a first step in matching client with jobs is by matching job classification codes.

Match "whole" client with "whole" employer

The successful agency uses this process only as the beginning. By considering other dimensions, they try to match the "whole client" with the "whole employer." Some of the considerations include:

    a. Quality of the job.

**Consider
job quality...**

Many agencies believe that few people are interested in low-paying, low-level, menial jobs which hold limited promise for advancement.

training...

b. Opportunities for training.
It is generally accepted that there is more interest in training now than in the past.

client interest...

c. Client's interest in the opportunity.
Some successful agencies believe that employer complaints about poor client motivation on the job stem from the agency's practice of placing clients in jobs that they never really wanted.

environment...

d. Company environment.
Many agencies believe that inexperienced, youthful clients feel more comfortable and may function better in smaller firms where individual attention and regard is commonplace.

**employer
personalities...**

e. Personalities of company staff.
The successful agency is likely to consider the personal values and preferences of the client along with those of the employer interviewer, and the potential employee's supervisor. The agency will try to select clients whose personality matches the employer's view of what a worker should be like.

job location

f. Location of the company.
Transportation is often a serious problem to consider. Where necessary, agencies are careful to refer clients only to employers easily accessible by public transportation or walking.

Throughout the Handbook you've been reading about the importance of really understanding what the employer's looking for. Your ability to contribute to a good employer/participant match depends on it. It's the acid test.

Getting Them Out The Door

Speed is of major concern in getting the client prepared for the interview. Once you determine whether or not the client is interested in the job, it is generally the agency that arranges the job interview.

Pre-placement briefings:

In some agencies, the pre-referral contact with the client is brief and minimal, often consisting of little more than, "This is the job. Are you interested?" Other agencies believe that careful attention should be devoted to preparing the client to meet the potential employer and doing well in the interview. This is much preferred. A pre-placement briefing is designed to fully inform the client of the "ins and outs" of the job and the employer, and to prepare them emotionally to succeed in the interview.

Prepare client for interview

The staff person who conducts the pre-placement briefing knows most of the employer's likes and dislikes. This individual may be the counselor, but normally it is the job developer who describes the job opportunity and its nuances. Topics covered in the briefing should include:

● job duties

● employer location

● transportation

● wages

● fringe benefits

● union information

● safety regulations

● likes and dislikes of the employer interviewer and supervisor

● the opportunity that exists for the participant

Bolster the client's confidence

Clients should have a chance to ask questions and request more information. Many agencies allow them to review the job description and make their own decisions about their interest in the job. Without painting an unrealistic picture of the job, you should attempt to bolster their confidence, enthusiasm and self-image.

While some agencies accompany clients to the interview, most rely on them going alone. RCA uses an appointment card which summarizes all of the employer location and contact information as well as the data and time of the interview. (A sample is reprinted at the end of this chapter.)

What Happened?

After the interview

Your follow up should be as soon after the interview as possible, because the results will initiate additional actions.

1. If the candidate was hired,

    a. employer thanks are in order, and

    b. employer/employee satisfaction should be monitored (see Chapter 8, Retention).

2. If the candidate was not hired,

    a. the agency must get another

qualified candidate in the employer's office as soon as possible, and

b. the candidate's ego and morale need attention.

It is up to you to find out

It will be up to you to find out whether or not the person was hired, and if not, why. Using the job order card, record all of the appropriate information:

1. Who was interviewed.

2. Date of interview.

3. What happened.

    a. Hired

    b. Not hired, and why

Note employer concerns

If the job opening still exists, note employer concerns on the card and return the job order to the pool. Work at translating employer objections like "too aggressive," into positive guidelines for selecting another candidate, such as "employer looking for non-aggressive, pleasant person who can work well with others."

Counsel the Client:

Job developers live with rejection on a daily basis so you can imagine how devastated the non-hired client feels. Your rejections aren't personal — the client's rejection seems very personal to him. Even failing an interview can be a valuable experience if it results in fuller self-understanding. When you carefully record the employer's responses to questions like, "what was right and what was wrong with the client," you can perform a vital counseling role, helping clients learn to eliminate the negatives and enhance the positives of their interviewing performance.

Turn rejection into positive experience

**Hold practice
interviews**

Some agencies use a trial-referral technique in which particularly cooperative employers conduct simulated interviews with clients. The employer works with the agency counselor to assess strengths and weaknesses, and suggest improvements. This information is then used to help clients improve their interviewing skills.

**Institute a
Shadow-Days
Program**

There are many reasons for not doing well in an interview, and one may very well be lack of interest. A Shadow-days Program can help people clarify their job interests by learning more about a particular occupation. Working with agency counselors, clients first research the activities and duties of an occupation. It is up to them to show an interest in learning more. If and when this happens, the agency arranges for them to spend time "shadowing" someone in that specific occupation.

Tie Up the Loose Ends

**Periodically
determine job
order status**

While follow up should occur immediately after someone has gone on an interview, you'll need some kind of back-up system to determine the status of all your job orders. A weekly check of your job order cards should take care of it. At VFI, for example, the back of each job order card is used to record what happened to each job order. Also, the board and job order box are updated weekly, with Board Cards and unfilled job orders returned to the appropriate job developer. Employers are called to determine whether or not the job is still open. If so, the cards are updated and recycled in the job pool.

Record Keeping

Agency records and tallies for contract requirements are accumulated from the job order cards. Job developers at VFI transfer the information onto back-up sheets, compiling monthly figures on clients referred on interviews, hired (full, part-time and temporary), jobs pending not used, and number of jobs developed.

Conclusion

In this chapter we've identified three particular areas in which organization and good management system will help you stay in control of the details:

1. Your employer list

   ● indexing, and regular contact

2. The job order information

   ● a standard form to help you record all the details

3. The referral and follow-up process

   ● job pooling

   ● weekly status checks on job orders

Take a few minutes to review the methods suggested here to determine whether or not they can be incorporated in your activities.

...Occasionally the process gets discouraging. There are many rude receptionists in this town who won't let job developers (or anyone else) talk to their bosses. There are employers who dump tales of woe (sometimes about young people's shortcomings) at great length. Every once in a while the burden of it all seems excessive. A quick run around the block followed by some refreshment does tend to restore equanimity and a sense of humor.

Veronica Anthony
Vocational Foundation, Inc.

JOB ORDER

DATE _____

JOB DEVELOPER _____

CO. _____ CONTACT _____ PHONE # _____

ADDRESS _____ NEAR _____ FLOOR _____

JOB TITLE _____ TYPE OF CO. or DEPT. _____ # OF OPENINGS _____

SALARY _____ HRS. _____ WK. EXP. _____

TYPE ( ) STENO ( ) DICTO. ( ) FIG. APT. ( ) PHONE ( ) ADD. MACH. ( ) DIPL. ( )

KEY INFORMATION

REFERRALS

STUDENT NAME	REG.	CLASS

RCA APPOINTMENT CARD

REGION_____CLASS_____

STUDENT_____

COMPANY_____

ADDRESS_____

RECRUITER_____PHONE #_____

INTERVIEW

DATE_____POSITION_____

TIME_____TIME RETURNED_____AM____PM_____

REFERRED BY:_____
            (212) 736-4445

8

Retention —
The Real Measure of Success

Overview

Job retention is often referred to in our business as the "bottom-line," because this is where the long-term gain will be measured. Since economic stability and a productive work force go hand in hand, our goals must focus on keeping people employed in worthwhile, satisfying jobs. Bottom-line retention, therefore, means reducing the kind of turnover which leads to labor-market dropouts.

Post-placement services most often receive the closest scrutiny whenever the question of retention comes up. However, since these services are generally an extension of the agency's overall approach, any attempts to improve retention should focus on the entire program. This chapter looks at all phases of agency services and highlights those areas that have direct impact on job retention. It also provides guidelines for developing a retention improvement plan within your agency.

A Myopic View Will Never Do

If the agency is to increase client job retention, every aspect of the service program must be designed to contribute to that goal. While it is common to look for solutions to the problem of low job retention by questioning post-placement services and staff members, the cause may well be a deficiency somewhere else in the agency's program.

The successful agency considers its program to be a three-phase sequence of services in

**Look at
all phases**

1. Pre-job placement
2. Placement
3. Post-job placement

all working together to promote job retention.

Pre-job Placement:

**Overall focus on
employer needs**

The overall nature of these services should focus on the expressed needs of employers. Your role in identifying and translating these needs into client programs has been previously stressed in Chapter 3.

Two services that can have a major impact on retention — Orientation to Work, and Counseling — are capsulized here.

**Include these
in orientation**

Orientation to Work — these topics are important:

● Dressing for the job*

● Work English and vocabulary*

● Job rules, regulations and behavior*

● Communicating at work*

● Handling hostility

● Giving and taking orders

● Interacting with fellow workers and supervisors*

● Setting and achieving goals

● Transportation systems

● Money management

As the most direct link between agency and employer you can provide specific information concerning employer expectations in these areas, especially those noted with asterisks.

Counseling tips

Counseling — Counselors have the potential for significant impact on clients, particularly youthful ones who may look to the experienced counselor as a mentor. As a job developer you should be aware of the following guidelines for counselors:

● Allow sufficient time for client sessions. An effective counselor must spend a great deal of time, energy, and personal attention with clients. (This is one reason for not having counselors also serve as job developers.)

● Have frequent, regular individual contacts with clients.

● Discuss the job in the context of the client's goals and aspirations. The clients should be aware that the job is a vehicle for achieving what is important to them.

● Be realistic about employment. Don't build the client's desire for a job to the extent that it becomes a disappointment.

● Concentrate on the particular employment problems of individual clients. These difficulties should be targeted quickly and treated as recurring problems with suggested better ways of working them out.

Placement

Concentrate on the best client-employer match

Placement services that concentrate on making a good match between client and employer will produce the best retention results. This has been previously stressed in Chapter 7, but the key points are summarized as follows:

● The agency should be concerned with matching the whole person with the whole employer. Successful agencies prepare full, detailed profiles on

Whole person/ whole employer

both client and employer which are used to match the client's assets with the employer's needs.

Variety of job choices

● Job developers should try to develop a variety of potential jobs to increase the clients' kinds of job choices.

Customized job development

● Job development should be customized or tailored in an attempt to match clients and employers. Customized job development is more sophisticated than job solicitation and requires special skills, patience, and extra effort on the part of the developer.

Develop specialized jobs

● Related to customized job development is the development of unusual or esoteric jobs in which clients may express an interest. From time to time, the agency will encounter a client who wishes to be placed in a type of job which the agency has never before developed. Rather than suggest that they accept a substitute (which is likely to create a job loss), the responsive agency will work to develop a job which really interests the client.

Client choice

● Clients should be given a voice in identifying job situations which interest them.

Conduct exit interviews

● Exit interviews should be conducted to find out why agency clients leave their jobs. Both the employer and client should be interviewed preferably by telephone, although a mailed questionnaire can be used.

Post-placement

Generally these activities fall into four categories:

1. Monitoring employer/employee satisfaction

2. Counseling

3. Supportive Services

4. Technical services

**Follow-up on
client performance**

1. Monitoring
Most agencies conduct a 30, 60, and 90 day follow-up after placement. Someone from the agency contacts the employer to determine if the client is still on the company payroll. In the case of a subsidized OJT job, this follow-up continues for the duration of the contract.

The follow-up procedure enables the agency to help both employer and client during the critical period of adjustment immediately after the client is hired. Regular, periodic follow-up is important in identifying and resolving problems before they grow serious. For this reason, some agencies provide a more concentrated follow-up, for example:

a. Contact with the employer and client immediately after the job interview.

b. A first after-hire follow-up with the employer and client within one, two or five days after the client has started the job.

c. A 30, 60, and 90 day follow-up, plus intermittent contacts in between.

d. An emphasis on easing the client's transition to the job, resolving conflicts that might threaten the job retention, and providing the necessary support which they require to sustain employment.

It is important that an agency be flexible and able to recognize individual differences between clients and employers. Some clients require intensive follow-up others are virtually trouble free and may not need a high degree of follow-up. These differences are true of employers as well. This judgment should be left to the person involved in the follow-up.

2. Counseling
The primary reason for post-placement counseling is to provide the necessary help that will reduce client-employer problems. The agency staff person who fills this role acts as a mediary to iron out any difficulties in the client's new job. Generally, this person: Has worked with and knows the client fairly well.

Reduce client-employer problems

● Provides personal support to the new employee as a field counselor.

● May work with the client outside of the work setting if necessary.

Watch for absenteeism and tardiness

Examples of the kinds of problems that need attention include: Absenteeism and tardiness.
The causes of these two most common problems may be quite varied, ranging from the client's simply not knowing that being absent can jeopardize his or her employment, to transportation difficulties, to far more complicated excuses. The client must be involved in identifying the cause and developing a solution to reduce the problem.

Involve client in problem-solving

    a. Loss of psychological orientation to work. This generic problem can encompass many others and is expressed when the client, sometimes suddenly, loses interest in the job or in continuing to work. The cause for the disenchantment must be found if you are going to help them solve the problem. It can be as simple as reassuring the client that he or she is well liked and accepted by others in the company. On the other hand, the problem and solution may be complex, difficult, and time consuming.

    b. Interpersonal difficulties.

Some clients have a difficult time adjusting to employment and particularly to the importance of working well with others. Some individuals experience difficulty handling the depersonalization that is part of assembly-line jobs.

c. Problems with supervisors.

The company supervisor can make or break the agency's post-placement program, even when the company is interested in working with the agency. If, for example, the supervisor does not want to release the employee for counseling during working hours, (a common occurrence), it may be necessary to arrange for it before or after working hours. It is important to show that these activities can resolve difficulties that supervisors may not want to be involved in, and that this extra effort can stabilize a supervisor's work force without interfering with production goals.

3. Supportive services.

In providing supportive services the agency is concerned with keeping the client on the job. Some supportive services come directly from the agency. Occasionally, the agency may suggest that they seek non-agency services, such as day-care centers, health services, emergency financial aid, transportation assistance, legal aid, housing assistance, and special counseling. Supportive services are usually provided or referred before job placement. If they are necessary after placement, the agency staff member responsible for follow-up helps the employee identify and secure the necessary services to avoid interrupting the client's employment.

Provide support, technical service

4. Technical services. The agency may also provide a selection of technical services which can be very helpful to the employer, enhancing the employer's acceptance and regard for the agency.

Usually it is the job developer who provides these extra services. For example, the job developer of the Rehabilitation Institute of Chicago (RIC) noticed that area employers were reluctant to hire the handicapped because, among other things, companies did not know what architectural changes should be made to their locations. The developer met with local architects, studied the field, and quickly achieved an expertise in the design field which was used to help employers improve their facilities.

Other areas of technical services in which the job developer may become involved include:

- Labor market information

- Affirmative action — EEO assistance

- Job analysis

- Advice on modifying jobs for the handicapped

- Wage rates and fringe benefits

- Hiring requirements

- Preparing job descriptions

- OJT specifications

- Working conditions

- Upgrading opportunities

- Government contracting opportunities available

- Supervisory-worker relations

- Occupational testing

- Measuring turnover and absenteeism

The job developer's involvement may be to secure and pass on information to the employer, refer the employer to sources of advice and guidance, or to work with the employer on a consulting basis. Whatever the form of assistance, by providing these technical services the developer can help to cement a relationship with employers, which is likely to produce increased numbers of job orders.

Cement a relationship with service

Changing Things for the Better

Constructing an improvement plan

Taking positive action to improve your agency's job retention rate requires the commitment and involvement of everyone in the agency. Use the following checkpoints as your guide when developing an improvement plan.

Get management support

☐ Support and a clear directive from agency management. Whether or not an agency is able to help clients retain their jobs depends a great deal on whether they have established job retention as a primary goal. This goal should be clearly stated by managers and widely communicated throughout the agency.

Select a planning committee

☐ A planning committee with representation from all levels and functions within the agency. This planning committee has the responsibility for fact—finding and developing the improvement plan. It should operate in the spirit of an open forum and encourage free exchange of ideas.

Working together to develop organizational goals and objectives allows everyone to see the big picture. This is especially important when everyone is usually immersed in the details of "getting the job done."

Steps in the Process

☐ **Fact-finding.**

1. Gather information about your existing program.

95

      a. review records and describe current retention situation.

      b. interview staff and clients to get a description of the "problem."

    2. Research a variety of retention programs used by other agencies.

☐ **Develop a Retention Improvement Plan.**

      a. Maintain a balance between desirable programs and the constraints of funding, current program priorities, and limitations of agency size and staff.

      b. Translate the program into identifiable and measurable objectives.

      c. Translate objectives into specific, written, staff responsibilities, activities, and accountability.

      d. Identify the specific steps necessary to change current operations. Remember that the steps should link all phases of agency services — from pre-placement through post-placement.

      e. Explain how the improvement program will be monitored, measured, and evaluated.

☐ **Implement, Evaluate, Modify**

This includes managerial review, and modification. Employer committees should be involved wherever possible. Implementation is everyone's responsibility. When the plan is developed by representatives from the entire agency it will be more easily accepted and put into effect. The same mutual effort that went in to developing the plan should be encouraged in its evaluation.

Remember that any improvement plan should be treated as a working document. When your objective is to effect change even your plan must allow for variation.

High Support: A Case Study

The following case study illustrates how extensive employer involvement can be used to improve job retention.

The High Support Program, operated by the Jobs Now Project in Chicago, has had proven success in reducing turnover. Recognizing that the transition period following placement is highly critical in terms of job retention, these job developers worked with employers to develop specific provisions for handling this period. They developed job programs, rather than job slots.

Job developers, called job program developers, worked through top-level people in the company to develop hiring and employment provisions. These provisions constituted a High Support Agreement, and addressed the following elements.

1. Lowered education requirements.
   With the agency's help, the employer would evaluate company entry-level hiring requirements and lower them where they were overly restrictive, outmoded, or unnecessary.

2. Individual consideration of police records. Most Jobs Now clients had had brushes with the law. In most cases, these police records were not serious or reflective of the person's capabilities or potential as an employee.

3. Lowered minimum standards on tests.

4. **Assignment of a co-worker as a buddy.**
   Under the buddy system an experienced worker teaches the new employee about the job, informal and formal company rules, and provides emotional support.

5. **After-placement and on-the-job** consultation between the client, the agency staff, and the client's supervisor.

6. **Notification of the agency if the client's performance falters.**
   At the first sign of potential trouble the employer would call the agency and together they would try to solve the difficulty.

7. **Conferring with the agency before discharging or taking punitive action against the client.** This "second chance" provision alone preserved many clients' jobs.

8. **Providing longer periods of orientation and training to placed clients.**

Jobs Now clients received only two weeks of pre-placement servicing — consisting of:

a. orientation to work

b. employment-oriented human relations training

c. instruction in resume preparation and applications.

The agency handled approximately 100 clients per each two-week cycle. After it had placed approximately 1,000 youths in approximately 200 companies, Jobs Now evaluated the relationship between the number of provisions accepted by a company and the incidence of job retention. There was a clear and positive relationship between job retention and the kinds of High Support provisions adhered to by employers. Companies with more than eight provisions experienced a retention rate averaging 73 percent. Companies which had instituted less than eight provisions had a turnover rate of 73 percent. The evaluation also showed that certain provisions had more impact on job success than others. These provisions were:

1. Post-placement consultation between agency staff and placed clients.

2. Cooperation between employers and agency staff members to improve the employee's performance on the job.

3. An employer-agency meeting before punitive action was taken against the employee.

4. Longer periods of orientation and training provided by employers.

Jobs Now worked with employers to develop additional in-company support programs, such as:

1. A seminar center to help company personnel learn to relate more humanely to their subordinates.

2. On-the-job orientation programs to assist the transition of clients to the job.

3. Training of company employees as counselors.

4. Aid to employers in developing on-the-job basic education programs, and consultation in designing in-company job training curricula.

5. Advice to employers in job restructuring and the development of viable career ladders for placed clients.

6. Identifying and training company buddies.

7. Advice in balancing extended training periods with actual work exposure.

8. Referring the company to supportive-services agencies in the community for use with troubled employees.

Many of the employers who worked with the agency still retain their programs, many of which have been amplified and refined. The concept continues to benefit disadvantaged workers more than a decade after its original development.

Conclusion

Every agency is required to report on retention. It is a key element in evaluating success, and one that everyone would like to improve. Does your agency view its program as a three-phase sequence of services in 1) pre-job placement, 2) placement, and 3) post-job placement?

Evaluate the strengths and weaknesses based on what you know of the agency operations, and discuss them with your manager. Together, list those things that could have a positive effect on retention which can be improved in the area of job development. Ask your manager about the feasability of a total agency improvement plan.

Appendix

The following agencies were among those visited during the research and fact-finding prior to the preparation of this Handbook.

Vocational Foundation, Inc.
44 East 23rd Street
New York, New York 10010

RCA Manpower & Career Development
Training Program
226 West 26th Street
New York, New York 10001

CABET (formerly CABMS)
201 North Wells
Chicago, Illinois 60606

Rehabilitation Institute of Chicago
345 East Superior
Chicago, Illinois 60606

Job Search Workshops, Inc.
1710 South Amphlett Boulevard
Suite 318
San Mateo, California 94402

Jobs for Youth (N.Y.-Boston-Chicago)
119 Charles Street
Boston, Massachusetts 02114

S.A.F.E.R. Foundation
10 South Wabash
Chicago, Illinois 60603